Note Reading Made FUN

with CD

Note Reading, Book 3

Kevin and Julia Olson

Production: Frank J. Hackinson
Production Coordinators: Peggy Gallagher and Philip Groeber
Editors: Edwin McLean and Peggy Gallagher
Cover and Interior Illustrations: Julia Olson
Engraving: Tempo Music Press, Inc.
Printer: Tempo Music Press, Inc.

THE F·J·H MUSIC COMPANY INC.
Frank J. Hackinson

ISBN-13: 978-1-61928-105-9

FJH2217

Table of Contents

Notes to the Teacher and Parent . . .

Piano Made FUN for the Young® is an early childhood piano curriculum designed to teach and reinforce the basics of piano study, in a spirit of FUN, PLAYFULNESS, and SUCCESS. The curriculum consists of *Sing-Along Activity Books* and leveled piano books with complimentary audio recordings. Notes and concepts are taught at a careful and steady pace, giving students a solid foundation without moving too quickly. It is especially effective in a group setting, but great for private students as well.

Young children enjoy lessons that offer a variety of experiences. This curriculum provides diverse learning opportunities that incorporate singing, movement, games, and more. A typical lesson is divided into two areas:

 **Rug Time**   ***Theory Made FUN; Counting Made FUN; Notes Made FUN***

During Rug Time, students sit on the floor near the piano and sing songs using the *Sing-Along Activity Books* to learn and review concepts. Singing the simple songs keeps their attention and helps them have fun while learning. Teachers who are not comfortable singing can use the recordings to listen to the songs with their students. Because the songs are short and easy to remember, many of them can be reviewed in a matter of minutes. **The beginning of each unit in the piano books indicates which concepts to cover at Rug Time.**

Piano Time   ***Pre-Reading Made FUN, Starter Book; Note Reading Made FUN, Book 1;***
Note Reading Made FUN, Book 2; Note Reading Made FUN, Book 3

During Piano Time, students use the leveled piano books with recordings to learn to play and read music at a pace that is steady and comfortable. The music is simple and easy to read so young students do not become frustrated. The themed units and play-along recordings make the learning process fun and interesting. (Each piece is recorded at a slow practice tempo; students may follow the indicated tempo and dynamic when ready.) The vocal parts have been recorded in appropriate vocal range and do not necessarily reflect the student's piano part.

Note Reading Made FUN, Book 3 is the fourth piano book used during Piano Time. It teaches and reinforces the notes in the G positions, F position, and D position. New notes are introduced at a steady and comfortable pace, with plenty of reinforcement. Each unit uses an animal theme—such as cows, dragons, and anteaters— to correlate with the new note introduced.

We are confident this curriculum will give young students an effective way to get started with the piano, in an atmosphere they can enjoy!

Remember, you can visit **www.PianoMadeFun.com** for free printables and teaching aids.

Kevin and Julia Olson

(signatures)

                                                              FJH2217

Practice Time at Home . . .

It is very important for parents to be willing to participate with daily practice time at home. You do not need to spend *much* time, but it is important to spend *some* time each day. Young students need careful supervision when they are first learning new pieces.

Here are a few suggestions for practice time at home:

Start out each practice session with a few songs from the *Sing-Along Activity Books.* (You may wish to use the recordings.) Check to see which unit your child's teacher has assigned for the week, and look at the beginning of that unit to find which songs to sing. You do not need to sing every song every day. Try to sing each song at least a few times per week, so your child can become familiar with the concepts. Young children enjoy singing the same songs over and over.

Once you have finished singing a few of the songs, move to the piano to help your child practice the pieces the teacher has assigned in *Note Reading Made FUN, Book 3.* Listen to the recording first, then help your child practice without the recording until they are ready to play with it. Encourage your child to practice each piece slowly and carefully, with nicely curved fingers. You may want to point along in the music as your child practices a new piece. Once he/she is comfortable, you won't need to point any longer.

Remember that young children need consistent reinforcement. You may even find that they sometimes forget something they have already learned. This is normal. Be patient and consistent and your child will eventually learn the pieces. It is also a good idea to consistently review old pieces. Just because your child has moved ahead in the book, does not mean he/she should stop playing the pieces he/she have already learned. This is a good time for your child to play the pieces along with the recordings. Young children love to play pieces that are comfortable to them, so go back and review pieces often.

Visit **www.PianoMadeFun.com** for more detailed instructions on how to help your child practice the pieces in this book. You can also go there for supplemental games and activities to do with your child at home.

Teacher Information for Rug Time . . .

The following pictures represent the new concepts that will be covered during Rug Time using the *Sing-Along Activity Books.* They are listed here for easy reference. It is not meant for students to memorize all of these concepts at once. Students will memorize and retain the information as they sing the songs and review them each week. The beginning of each unit will indicate which concepts to cover for that unit.

You will see that all of the concepts in the *Theory Made FUN* and *Counting Made FUN* books have been introduced at this point. It is suggested that teachers continue to rotate and review the concepts in these books each week at Rug Time. Young children enjoy the process of reviewing concepts previously learned. Doing so will help increase comprehension, build confidence and self-esteem, and provide a solid foundation for learning. You can visit **www.PianoMadeFun.com** for resources to use at Rug Time.

CHOOSE AND REVIEW
AS DESIRED.

CHOOSE AND REVIEW
AS DESIRED.

FJH2217

FJH2217

Low G Hand Position for Left Hand . . .

The first group of notes in this book are with the right hand in Middle C Position and the left hand in Low G Position. To play with the left hand in Low G Position, place the left-hand thumb on Duck Note D. Place the rest of your fingers as indicated in the guide below.

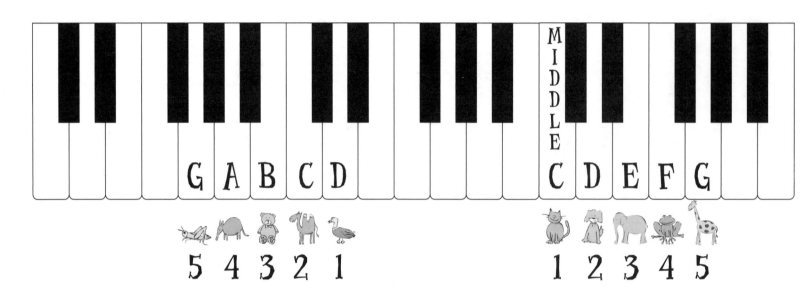

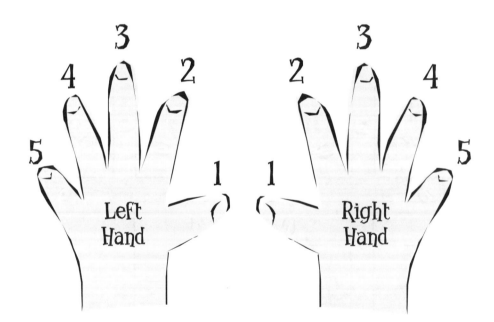

Remember hand positions are only "guides" that help you feel comfortable learning new notes. Once you are comfortable, your teacher can help you explore your pieces further by starting on a different finger.

FJH2217

Getting Comfortable in Low G Position . . .

Practice playing the right-hand notes in the Middle C position, then practice playing the left-hand notes in the Low G Position. With one hand at a time, place your fingers in position, then play each note going up, then going down as shown with the animal pictures below. The finger numbers are there to guide you. You can play this as a warm-up every day for practice time at home.

Right Hand

Left Hand

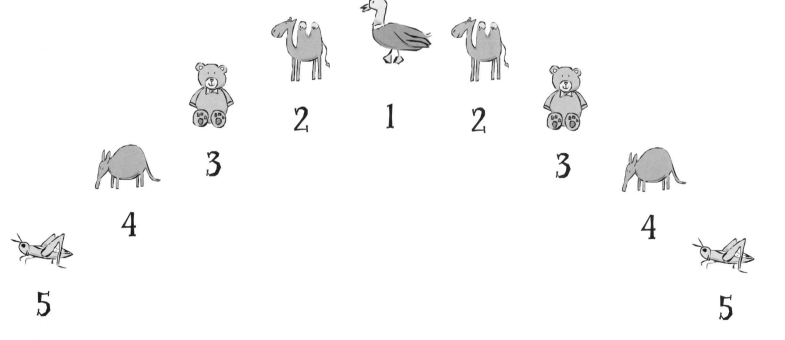

UNIT 1

Theory Made FUN Sing-Along Book. Choose and review as desired.
Counting Made FUN Sing-Along Book. Choose and review as desired.
Notes Made FUN Sing-Along Book. tracks 1-5, 19-23.

Piano Time

Duck Note D and Camel Note C

Review DUCK NOTE D AND CAMEL NOTE C ON THE KEYBOARD:
Find and play Duck Note D and Camel Note C on the keyboard. This time, play Duck Note D with L.H.
finger 1 and play Camel Note C with L.H. finger 2.

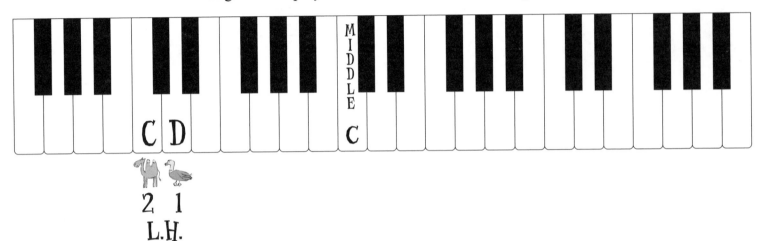

Review DUCK NOTE D AND CAMEL NOTE C ON THE STAFF:

Play the example below, keeping your eyes on the music.

1. Name notes:	D	C	D	C	D	D	D	D	D	C	D	C	D			
2. Count:	1	2	3	4	1	2	3	4	1	2	3	4	1	2	3	4

FJH2217

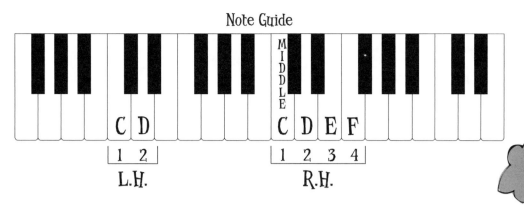

Note Guide

Lincoln Park Zoo

Andante

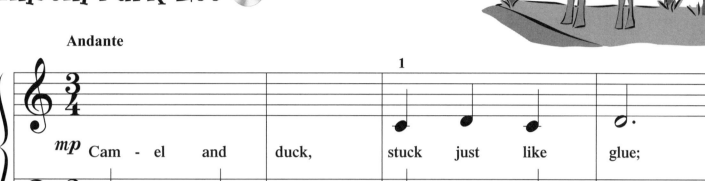

mp Cam - el and duck, stuck just like glue;

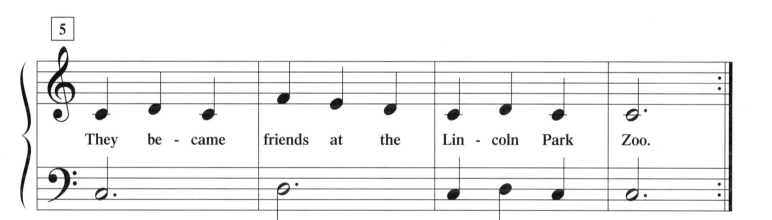

They be - came friends at the Lin - coln Park Zoo.

Teacher Duet: Student plays one octave higher.

ped. simile

Bear Note B

BEAR NOTE B ON THE KEYBOARD:
Find and play all of the B's on your piano. Now find the B that sits below Camel Note C.
We will call it Bear Note B for fun. You can play Bear Note B with L.H. finger 3.

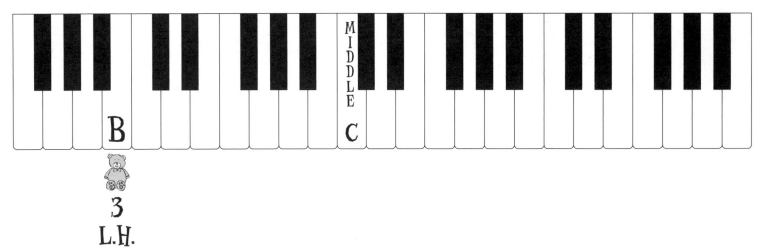

BEAR NOTE B ON THE STAFF:
Bear Note B sits on line number 2 of the bass staff.

Play the example below, keeping your eyes on the music.

1. Name notes:	C	D	C	B	C	D	C	B	C	D	C	B	C			
2. Count:	1	2	3	4	1	2	3	4	1	2	3	4	1	2	3	4

FJH2217

Note Guide

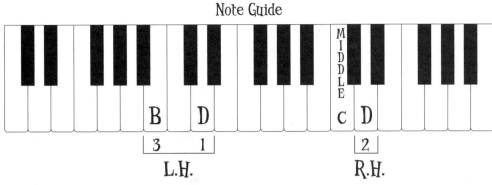

Not Afraid of Me 2

Andante

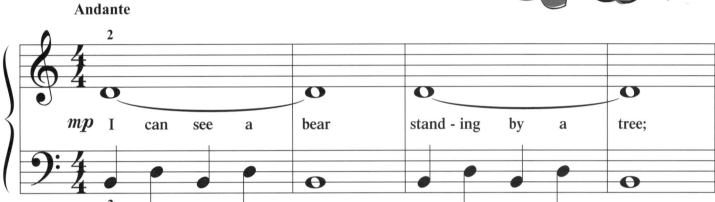

mp I can see a bear stand - ing by a tree;

When played as a solo, press the right (damper) pedal for the entire piece.

5

I'm a - fraid of him, but he's not a - fraid of me.

Teacher Duet: Student plays one octave higher.

Play 8va lower throughout

Anteater A

ANTEATER A ON THE KEYBOARD:

Find and play all of the A's on your piano. Now find the A that sits below Bear Note B.
We will call it Anteater A for fun. You can play Anteater A with L.H. finger 4.

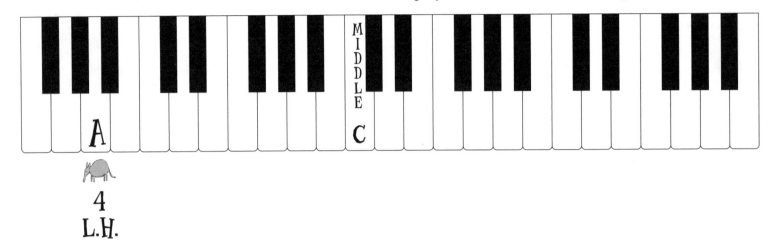

ANTEATER A ON THE STAFF:

Anteater A sits on space number 1 of the bass staff.

Play the example below, keeping your eyes on the music.

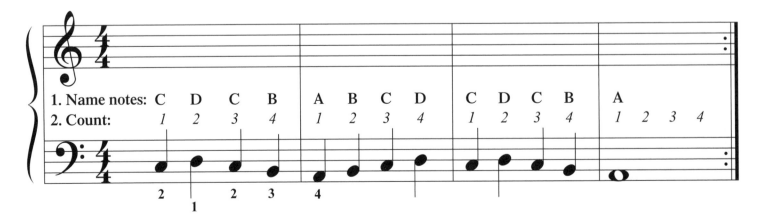

1. Name notes:	C	D	C	B	A	B	C	D	C	D	C	B	A			
2. Count:	*1*	*2*	*3*	*4*	*1*	*2*	*3*	*4*	*1*	*2*	*3*	*4*	*1*	*2*	*3*	*4*

FJH2217

Note Guide

What Do You Eat? 3

Allegro

mp Ant - eat - er, ant - eat - er, what do you eat?

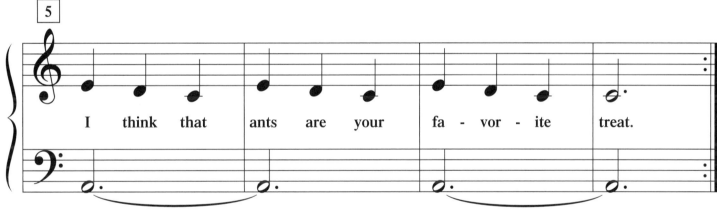

5

I think that ants are your fa - vor - ite treat.

Teacher Duet: Student plays one octave higher.

L.H. *p*

ped. simile

5

Grasshopper G

GRASSHOPPER G ON THE KEYBOARD:
Find and play all of the G's on your piano. Now find the G that sits below Anteater A.
We will call it Grasshopper G for fun. You can play Grasshopper G with L.H. finger 5.

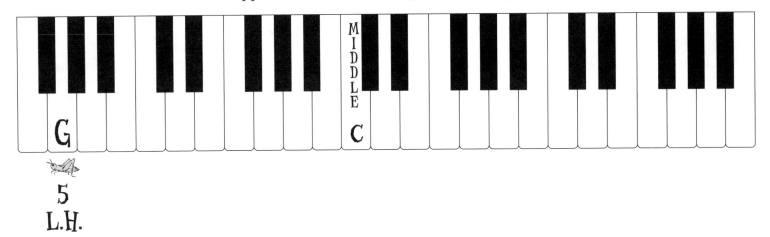

GRASSHOPPER G ON THE STAFF:
Grasshopper G sits on line number 1 of the bass staff.

Play the example below, keeping your eyes on the music.

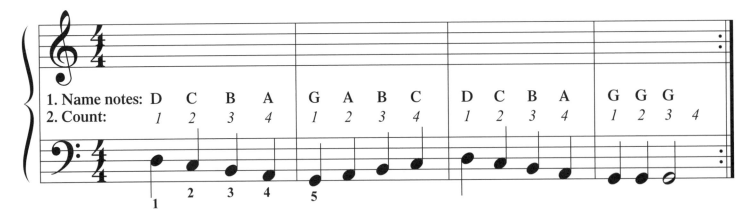

1. Name notes:	D	C	B	A		G	A	B	C		D	C	B	A		G G G
2. Count:		1	2	3	4	1	2	3	4		1	2	3	4		1 2 3 4

FJH2217

Note Guide

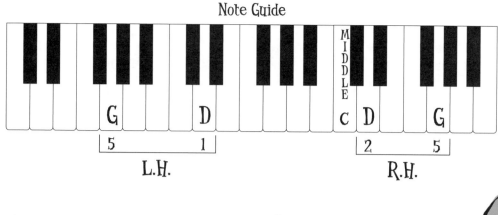

Grasshopper Hops 🔘4

Andante

f Grass - hop - per | hops on the | grass and the | rocks; He

5

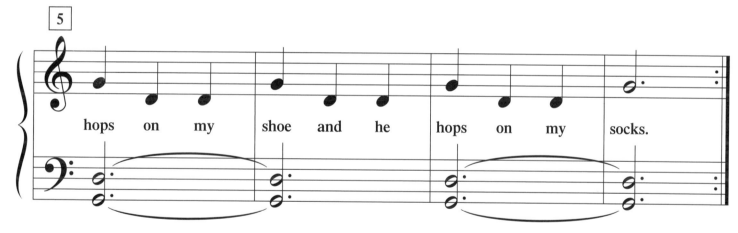

hops on my | shoe and he | hops on my | socks.

Teacher Duet: Student plays as written.

Play 8va higher throughout

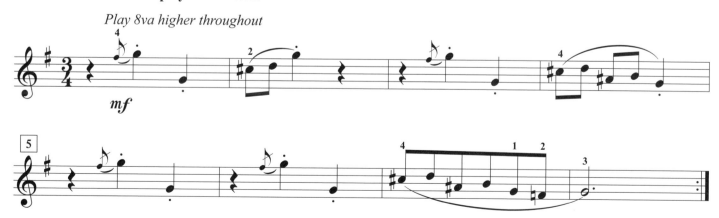

mf

G Hand Position . . .

The next group of notes in this book are with the left hand in Low G Position and the right hand in G Position. To play with the right hand in G Position, place the right-hand thumb on Giraffe Note G. Place the rest of your fingers as indicated in the guide below.

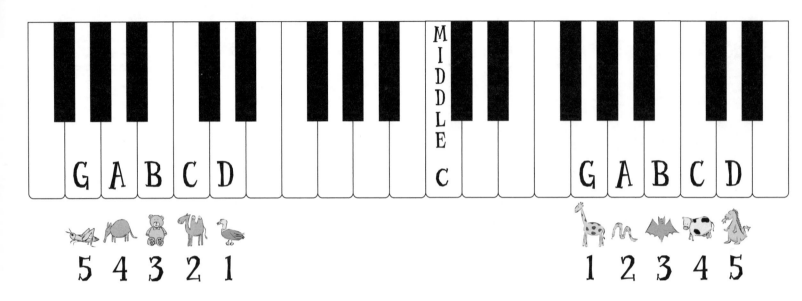

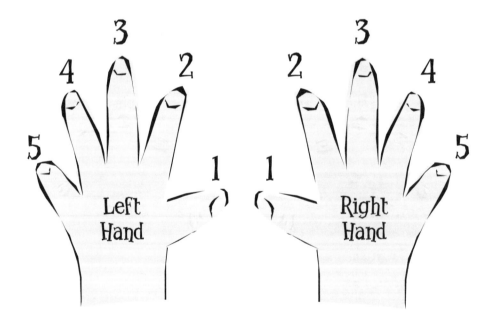

Remember hand positions are only "guides" that help you feel comfortable learning new notes. Once you are comfortable, your teacher can help you explore your pieces further by starting on a different finger.

FJH2217

Getting Comfortable in G Position . . .

Review playing the left-hand notes in Low G Position, then practice playing the right-hand notes in the G Position. With one hand at a time, place your fingers in position, then play each note going up, then going down as shown with the animal pictures below. The finger numbers are there to guide you. You can play this as a warm-up every day for practice time at home. Try playing hands together when you feel ready.

Right Hand

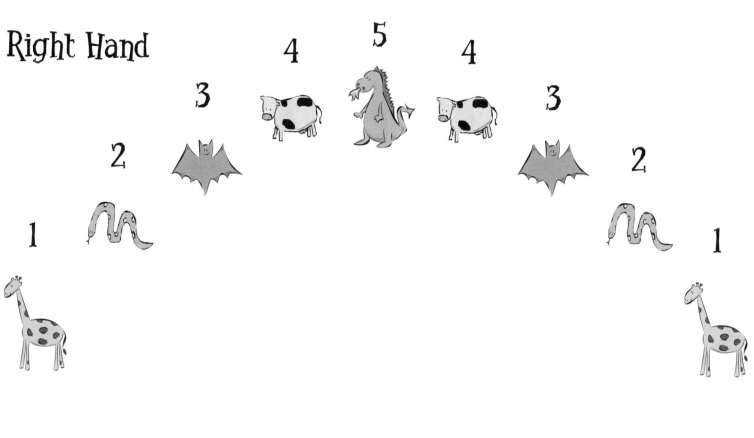

Left Hand

UNIT 2  Rug Time

Theory Made FUN Sing-Along Book. Choose and review as desired.
Counting Made FUN Sing-Along Book. Choose and review as desired.
Notes Made FUN Sing-Along Book tracks 5-7, 19-23.

 **Piano Time**

Giraffe Note G

Review GIRAFFE NOTE G ON THE KEYBOARD:
Find and play Giraffe Note G on your piano. This time, play Giraffe Note G with R.H. finger 1.

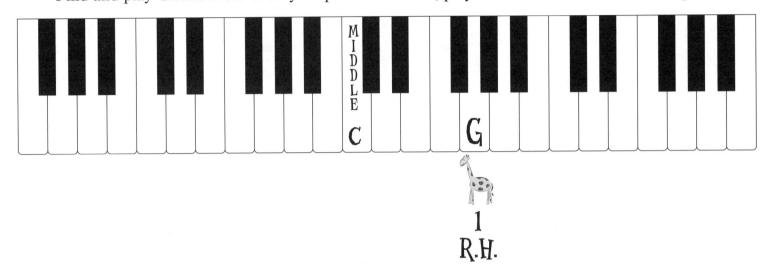

Review GIRAFFE NOTE G ON THE STAFF:

Play the example below, keeping your eyes on the music.

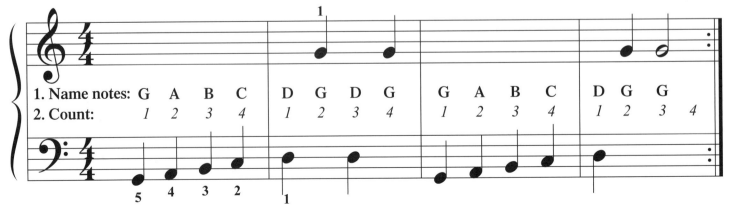

1. Name notes:	G	A	B	C	D	G	D	G	G	A	B	C	D	G	G
2. Count:	*1*	*2*	*3*	*4*	*1*	*2*	*3*	*4*	*1*	*2*	*3*	*4*	*1*	*2*	*3*	*4*

FJH2217

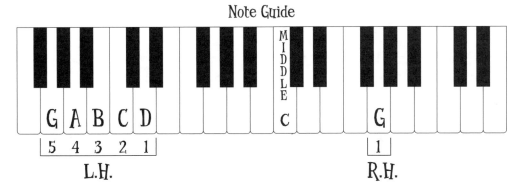

Note Guide

Such a Crazy Ride

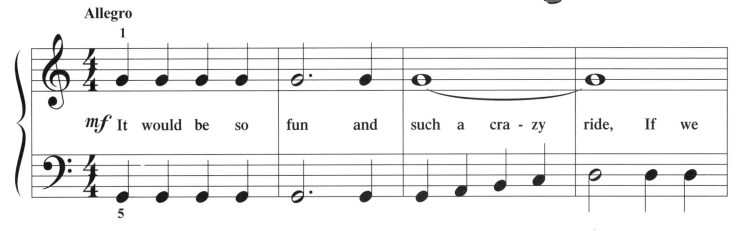

Allegro

mf It would be so fun and such a cra-zy ride, If we

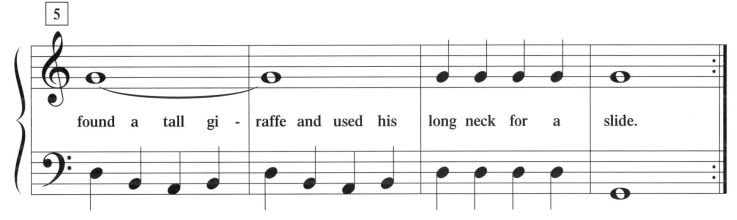

5

found a tall gi - raffe and used his long neck for a slide.

Teacher Duet: Student plays one octave higher.

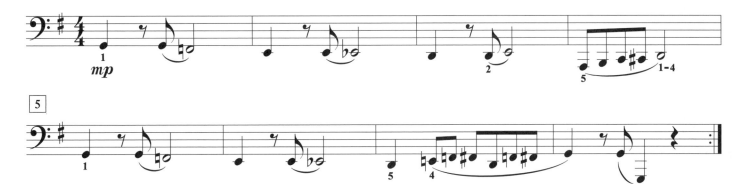

Anaconda A

ANACONDA A ON THE KEYBOARD:
Find and play all of the A's on your piano. Now find the A that sits above Giraffe Note G.
We will call it Anaconda A for fun. You can play Anaconda A with R.H. finger 2.

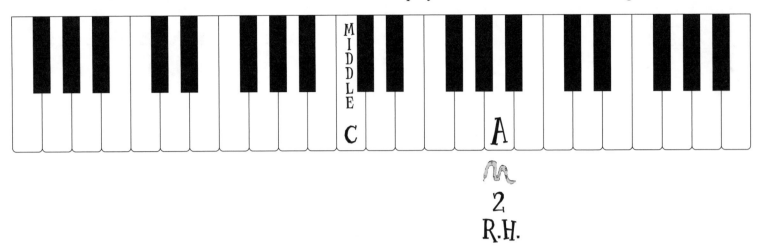

ANACONDA A ON THE STAFF:
Anaconda A sits on space number 2 of the treble staff.

Play the example below, keeping your eyes on the music.

1. Name notes:	G	A	G	A	G	G	A	A	G	A	G	A	G			
2. Count:	*1*	*2*	*3*	*4*	*1*	*2*	*3*	*4*	*1*	*2*	*3*	*4*	*1*	*2*	*3*	*4*

FJH2217

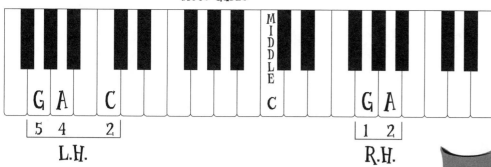

Giant Snake

Largo

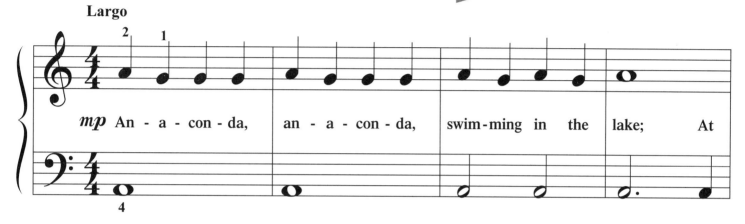

mp An - a - con - da, an - a - con - da, swim-ming in the lake; At

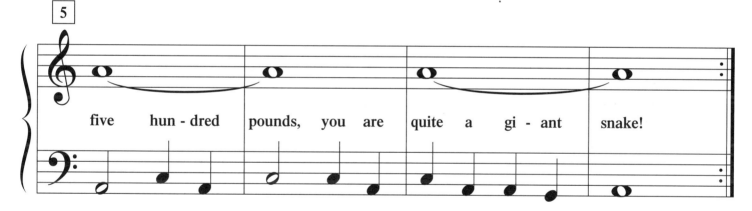

five hun - dred pounds, you are quite a gi - ant snake!

Teacher Duet: Student plays one octave higher.

Bat Note B

BAT NOTE B ON THE KEYBOARD:
Find and play all of the B's on your piano. Now find the B that sits above Anaconda A.
We will call it Bat Note B for fun. You can play Bat Note B with R.H. finger 3.

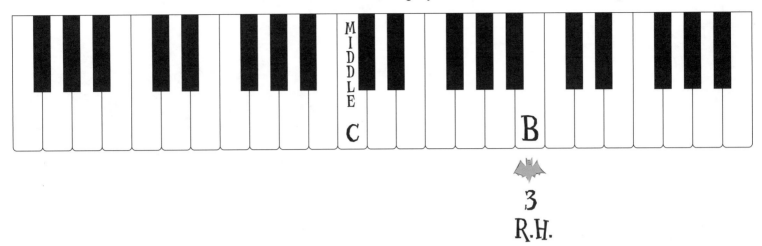

BAT NOTE B ON THE STAFF:
Bat Note B sits on line number 3 of the treble staff.

Play the example below, keeping your eyes on the music.

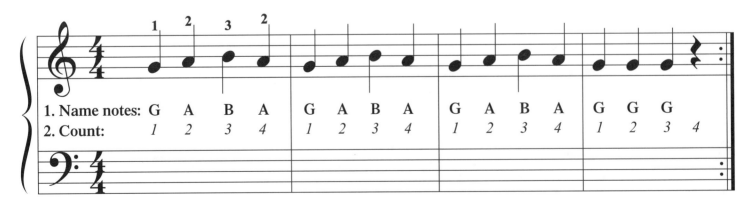

1. Name notes:	G	A	B	A	G	A	B	A	G	A	B	A	G	G	G
2. Count:	*1*	*2*	*3*	*4*	*1*	*2*	*3*	*4*	*1*	*2*	*3*	*4*	*1*	*2*	*3*	*4*

FJH2217

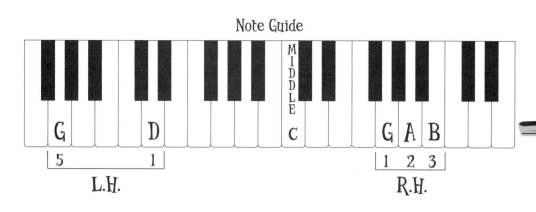

Note Guide

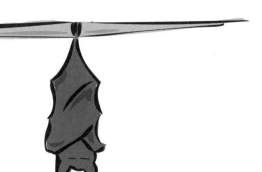

Hanging Upside Down 7

Andante

mp See the big black bat nap - ping just like that:

Wings that wrap a - round his bod - y hang - ing up - side down.

Teacher Duet: Student plays as written.

Play 8va higher throughout

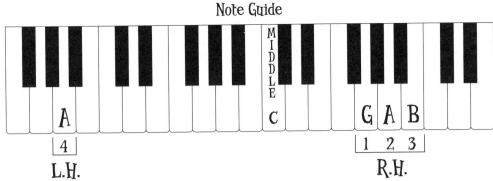

Note Guide

Take Flight 🔘8

Allegro

mf Watch the bat take flight | in the dark of | night;

5

See his wings flap | rap - id - ly a - | cross the moon so | bright.

Teacher Duet: Student plays one octave higher.

mp
with pedal

FJH2217

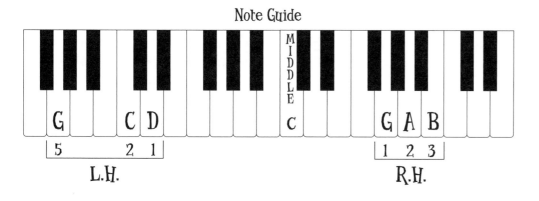

Note Guide

Frightening 🔟 9

Andante

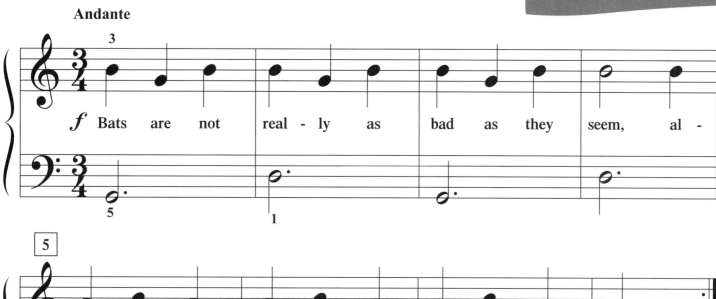

f Bats are not real - ly as bad as they seem, al -

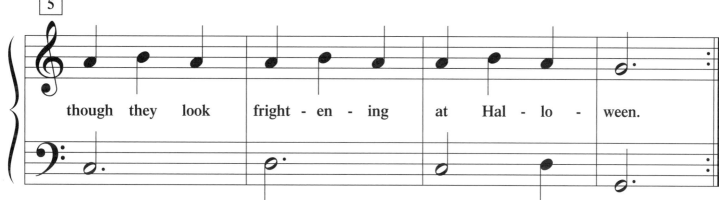

though they look fright - en - ing at Hal - lo - ween.

Teacher Duet: Student plays as written.

UNIT 3  Rug Time

Theory Made FUN Sing-Along Book. Choose and review as desired.
Counting Made FUN Sing-Along Book. Choose and review as desired.
Notes Made FUN Sing-Along Book tracks 5-9, 19-23.

Piano Time

Cow Note C

COW NOTE C ON THE KEYBOARD:
Find and play all of the C's on your piano. Now find the C that sits above Bat Note B.
We will call it Cow Note C for fun. You can play Cow Note C with R.H. finger 4.

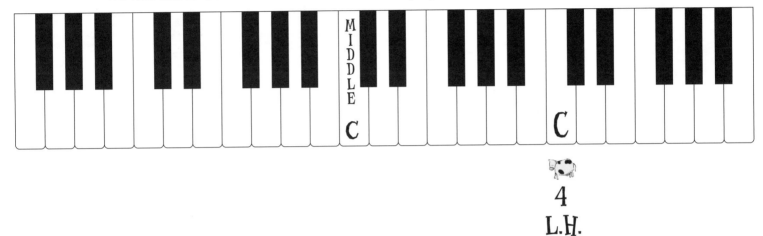

COW NOTE C ON THE STAFF:
Cow Note C sits on space number 3 of the treble staff.

Play the example below, keeping your eyes on the music.

1. Name notes:	G	A	B	C	G	A	B	C	G	A	B	C	C
2. Count:	1	2	3	4	1	2	3	4	1	2	3	4	1 2 3 4

FJH2217

Note Guide

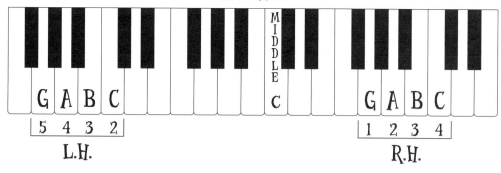

Rest in the Sun

Andante

mp Black and white | cow likes to | rest in the | sun; She

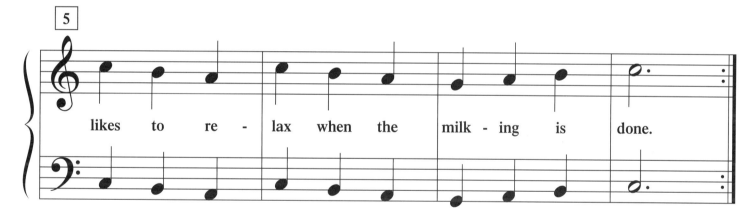

likes to re - | lax when the | milk - ing is | done.

Teacher Duet: Student plays one octave higher.

p

with pedal

Dragon Note D

DRAGON NOTE D ON THE KEYBOARD:
Find and play all of the D's on your piano. Now find the D that sits above Cow Note C.
We will call it Dragon Note D for fun. You can play Dragon Note D with R.H. finger 5.

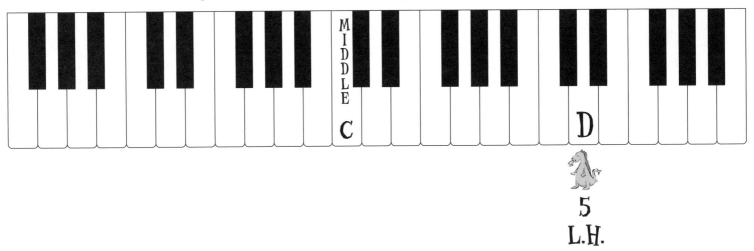

DRAGON NOTE D ON THE STAFF:
Dragon Note D sits on space line number 4 of the treble staff.

Play the example below, keeping your eyes on the music.

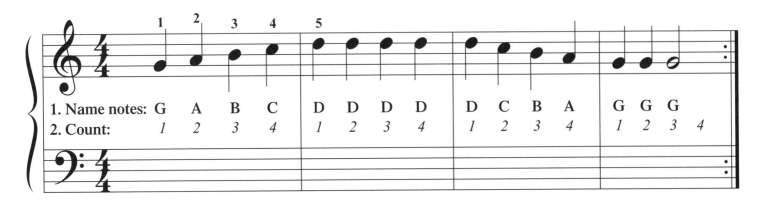

| 1. Name notes: | G | A | B | C | D | D | D | D | D | C | B | A | G | G | G | |
| 2. Count: | 1 | 2 | 3 | 4 | 1 | 2 | 3 | 4 | 1 | 2 | 3 | 4 | 1 | 2 | 3 | 4 |

FJH2217

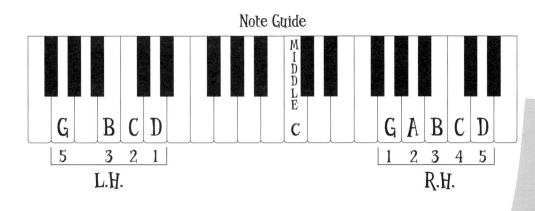

Enjoying the Breeze 🔘 11

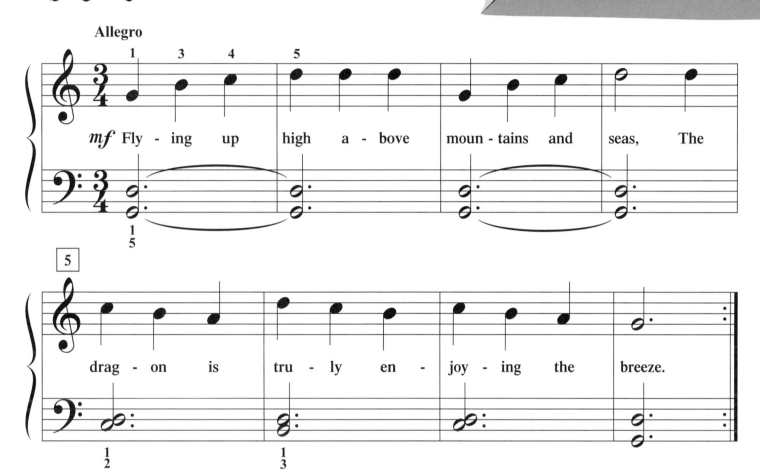

Allegro

mf Fly - ing up high a - bove moun - tains and seas, The

drag - on is tru - ly en - joy - ing the breeze.

Teacher Duet: Student plays as written.

Play 8va higher throughout

mp

with pedal

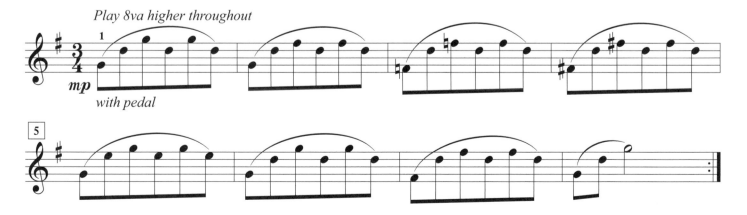

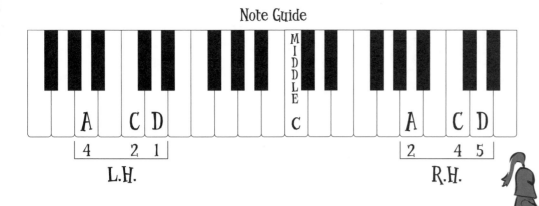

Note Guide

Big Surprise? 12

Largo

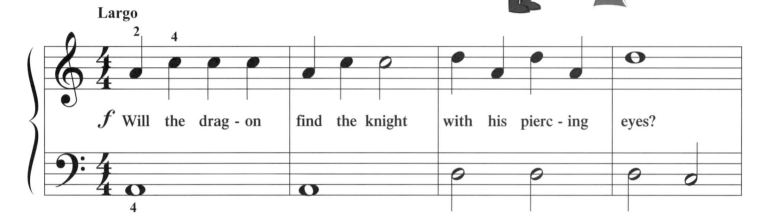

f Will the drag - on | find the knight | with his pierc - ing | eyes?

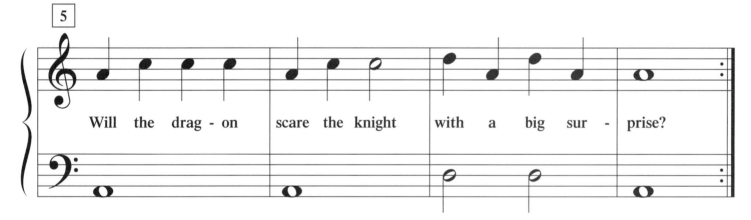

Will the drag - on | scare the knight | with a big sur - prise?

Teacher Duet: Student plays as written.

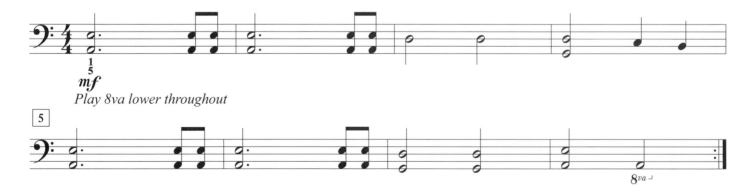

mf
Play 8va lower throughout

FJH2217

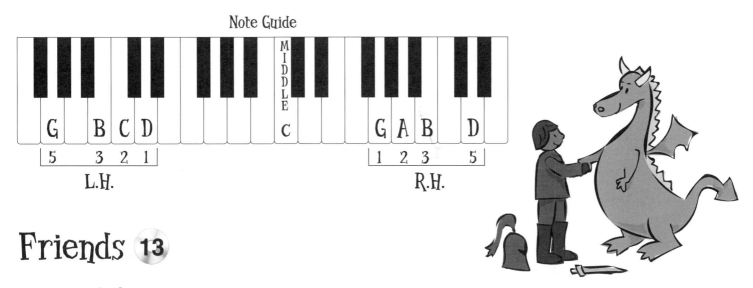

Note Guide

Friends 13

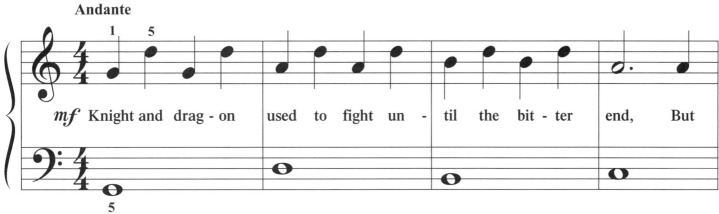

Andante

mf Knight and drag - on used to fight un - til the bit - ter end, But

they de - cid - ed it would be much bet - ter to be friends.

Teacher Duet: Student plays one octave higher.

Play 8va lower throughout

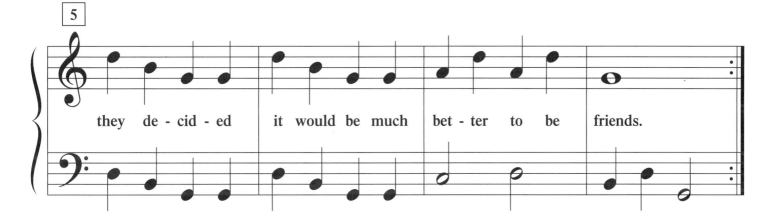

mp *with pedal*

Treble G Hand Position . . .

The next group of notes in this book are in Treble G Position. To play in Treble G Position, place the left-hand thumb on the D above Middle C. This note is actually Dog Note D, but this time you will play it with left hand. Place the right-hand thumb on the G above Middle C. Place the rest of your fingers as indicated in the guide below.

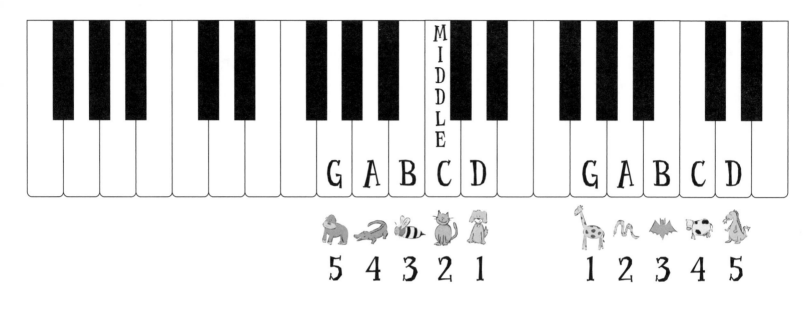

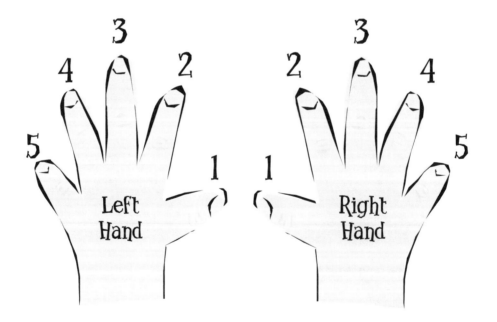

Remember hand positions are only "guides" that help you feel comfortable learning new notes. Once you are comfortable, your teacher can help you explore your pieces further by starting on a different finger.

FJH2217

Getting Comfortable in Treble G Position . . .

Review playing the right-hand notes in the G Position, then practice playing the left-hand notes in the Treble G Position. With one hand at a time, place your fingers in position, then play each note going up, then going down as shown with the animal pictures below. The finger numbers are there to guide you. You can play this as a warm-up every day for practice time at home. Try playing hands together when you feel ready.

Right Hand

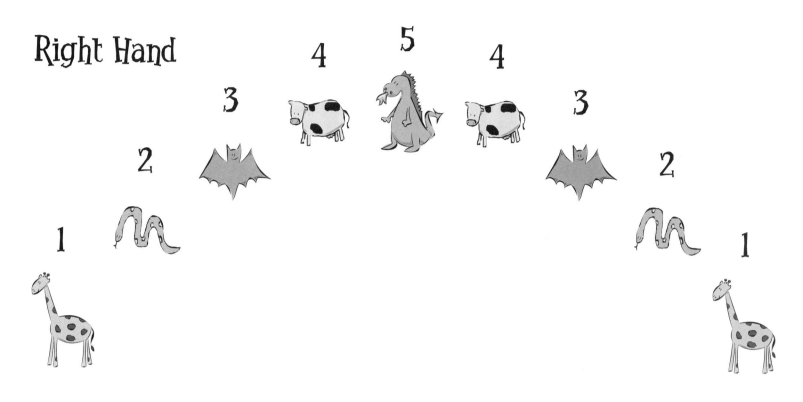

Left Hand

UNIT 4  Rug Time

Theory Made FUN Sing-Along Book. Choose and review as desired.
Counting Made FUN Sing-Along Book. Choose and review as desired.
Notes Made FUN Sing-Along Book tracks 5-9, 13-16.

Piano Time

Dog Note D and Cat Note C

Review DOG NOTE D AND CAT NOTE C ON THE KEYBOARD:
Find and play Dog Note D and Cat Note C on your piano. This time, play Dog Note D
with L.H. finger 1 and play Cat Note C with L.H. finger 2.

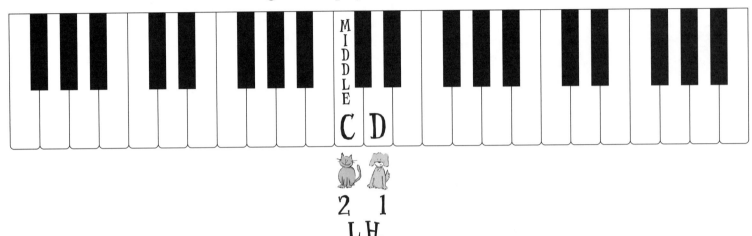

DOG NOTE D AND CAT NOTE C ON THE BASS STAFF:
Notice that Dog Note D sits in the space above Cat Note C on the bass staff in this position.

Play the example below, keeping your eyes on the music.

1. Name notes:	D	C	D	C		D	D	C	C		D	C	D	C		D			
2. Count:	1	2	3	4		1	2	3	4		1	2	3	4		1	2	3	4

FJH2217

Note Guide

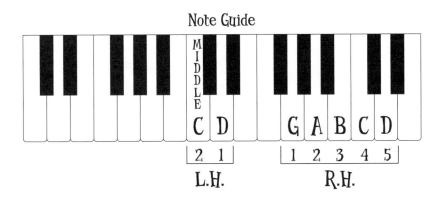

The Sappy Tree 14

Andante

𝑓 Cat and dog both | take a nap | by a tree that's | drip-ping sap.

5

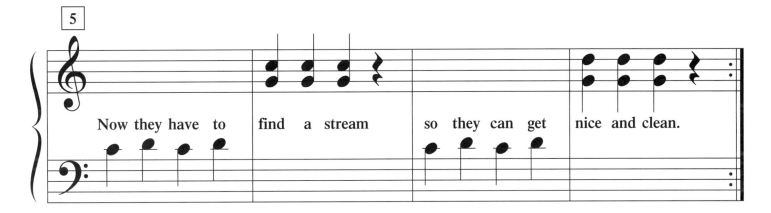

Now they have to | find a stream | so they can get | nice and clean.

Teacher Duet: Student plays as written.

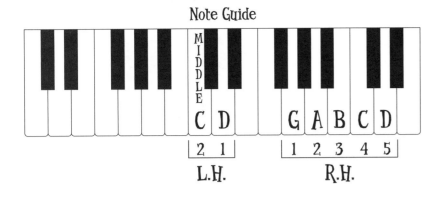

Note Guide

Stargazing 15

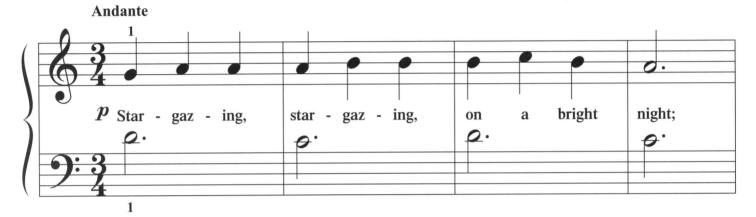

Andante

p Star - gaz - ing, star - gaz - ing, on a bright night;

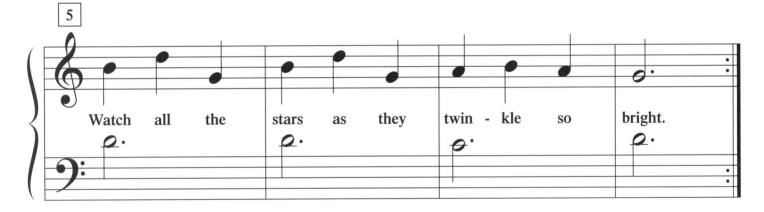

Watch all the stars as they twin - kle so bright.

Teacher Duet: Student plays as written.

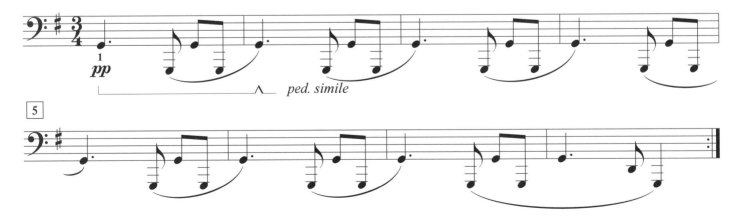

pp

ped. simile

Note Guide

Boring Day 🔘16

Largo

mf It's a long and bor - ing day, with noth - ing much to do;

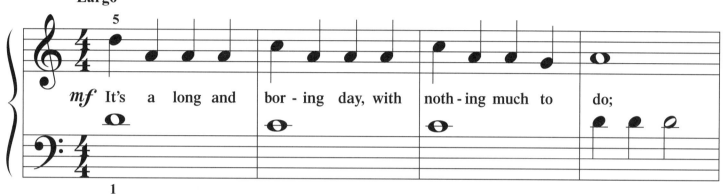

5

May - be cat can find a toy and dog can find a shoe.

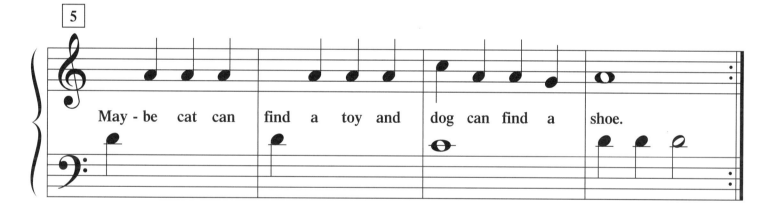

Teacher Duet: Student plays as written.

R.H.

L.H. *mp*

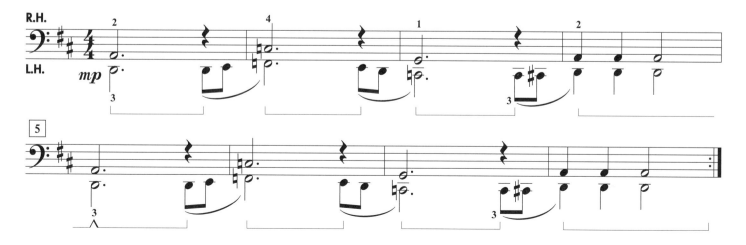

5

Bee Note B, Alligator A, and Gorilla Note G

Review BEE NOTE B, ALLIGATOR A, and GORILLA NOTE G ON THE KEYBOARD:
Find and play Bee Note B, Alligator A, and Gorilla Note G on your keyboard. This time, play Bee Note B
with L.H. finger 3, play Alligator A with L.H. finger 4 and play Gorilla Note G with L.H. finger 5.

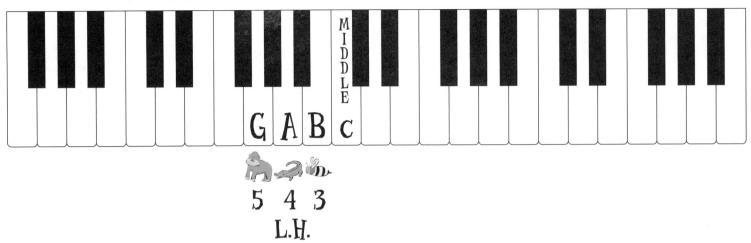

Review BEE NOTE B, ALLIGATOR A, and GORILLA NOTE G ON THE STAFF:

Play the example below, keeping your eyes on the music.

1. Name notes:	D	C	B	A	G	A	B	C	D	C	B	A	G	G	G	
2. Count:	*1*	*2*	*3*	*4*	*1*	*2*	*3*	*4*	*1*	*2*	*3*	*4*	*1*	*2*	*3*	*4*

1 2 3 4   5

Note Guide

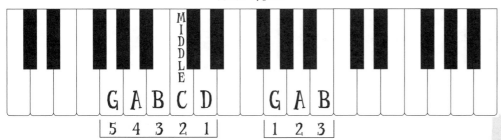

Sunny Sunday 17

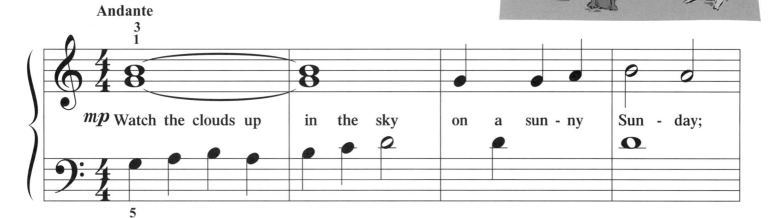

Andante

mp Watch the clouds up | in the sky | on a sun - ny | Sun - day;

See the birds all | fly - ing by, | on their way to | Mon - day.

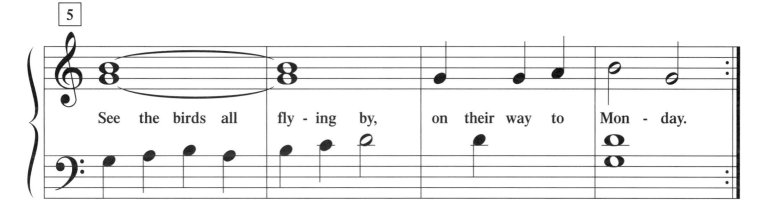

Teacher Duet: Student plays as written.

Play 8va higher throughout

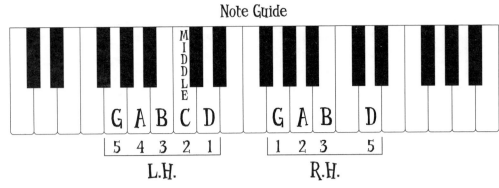

Note Guide

Green Balloon 🔘18

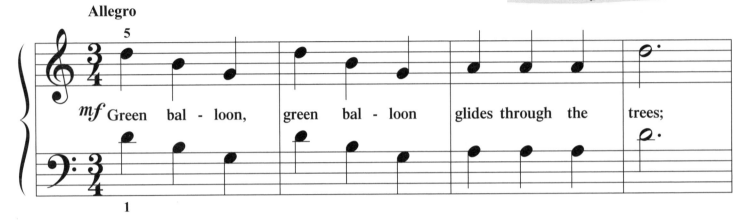

Allegro

mf Green bal - loon, green bal - loon glides through the trees;

Green bal - loon, green bal - loon flies with the breeze.

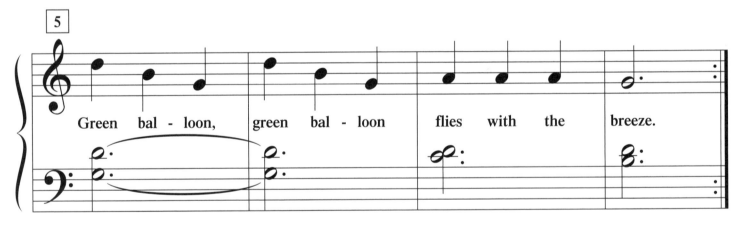

Teacher Duet: Student plays one octave higher.

mp
with pedal

FJH2217

Note Guide

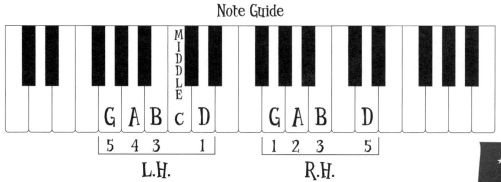

Moonlight

Andante

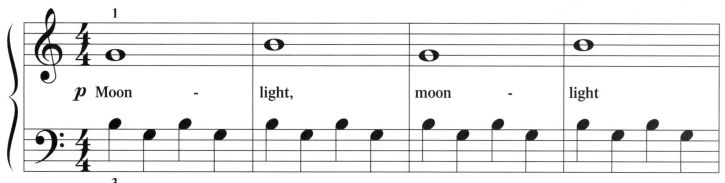

p Moon - light, moon - light

When played as a solo, press the right (damper) pedal for the entire piece.

5

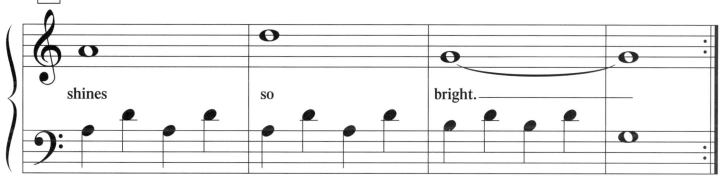

shines so bright.

Teacher Duet: Student plays as written.

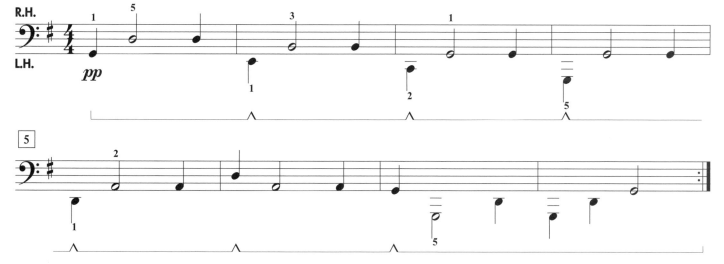

pp

F Hand Position . . .

The next group of notes in this book are in F Position. To play in F Position, place the left-hand thumb on Middle C and finger number 2 on the BLACK KEY just to the left of B. This note is called B flat and we will call it Bee Note B Flat for fun. Place the right-hand thumb on Frog Note F and place finger number 4 on the higher B flat. We will call that note Bat Note B Flat for fun. Place the rest of your fingers as indicated in the guide below.

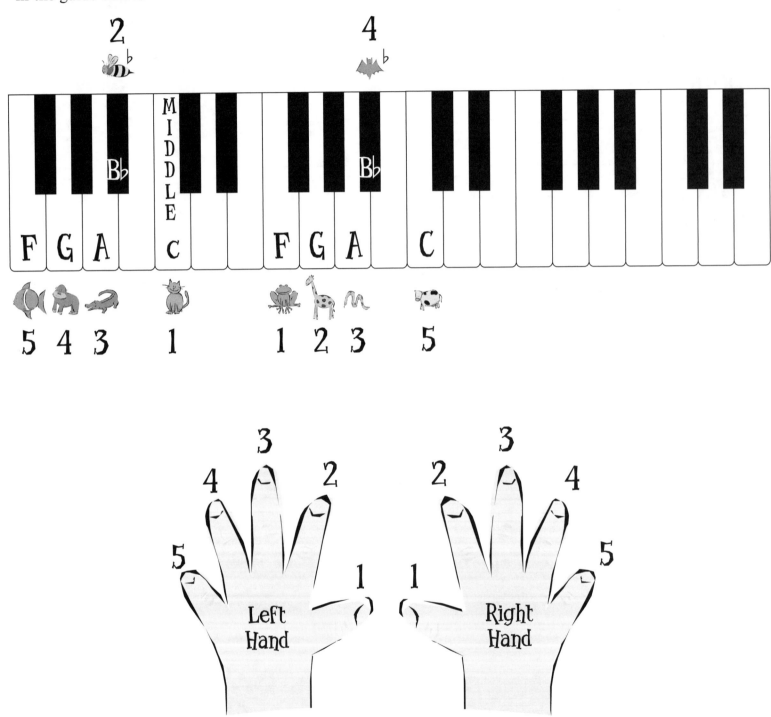

Remember hand positions are only "guides" that help you feel comfortable learning new notes. Once you are comfortable, your teacher can help you explore your pieces further by starting on a different finger.

                                                                FJH2217

Getting Comfortable in F Position . . .

Practice playing the notes in F Position. With one hand at a time, place your fingers in position, then play each note going up, then going down as shown with the animal pictures below. The finger numbers are there to guide you. You can play this as a warm-up every day for practice time at home. Try playing hands together when you feel ready.

Right Hand

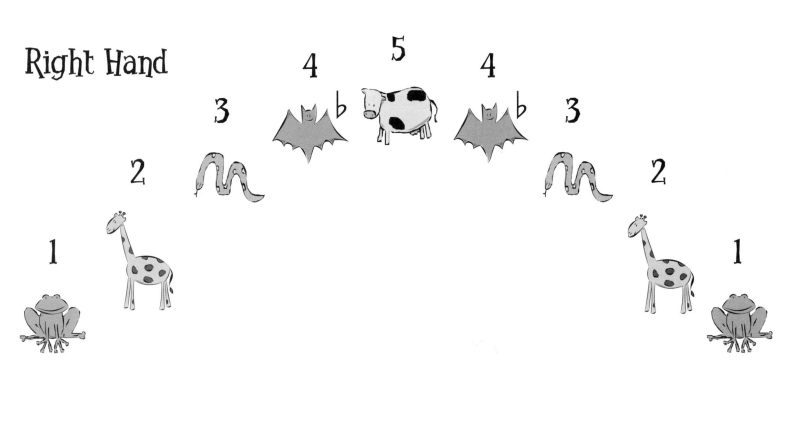

Left Hand

UNIT 5

Theory Made FUN Sing-Along Book. Choose and review as desired.
Counting Made FUN Sing-Along Book. Choose and review as desired.
Notes Made FUN Sing-Along Book tracks 4-8, 13-17.

F Position Animals
on the Bass Staff

CAT NOTE C, BEE NOTE B FLAT, ALLIGATOR A, GORILLA NOTE G, and FISH NOTE F:
Find and play Cat Note C, Bee Note B Flat, Alligator A, Gorilla Note G, and Fish Note F on your piano.
Remember to play with your L.H. finger 2 on the black key that sits just to the LEFT of Bee Note B.

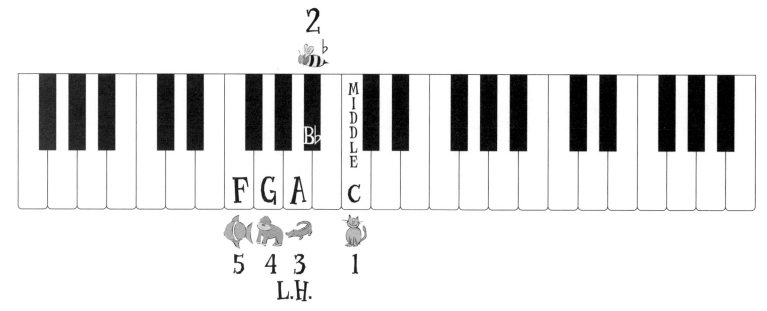

CAT NOTE C, BEE NOTE B FLAT, ALLIGATOR A, GORILLA NOTE G, and FISH NOTE F
ON THE BASS STAFF:

Play the example below, keeping your eyes on the music.

1. Name notes:	C	B♭	A	G		F	G	A	B♭		C	B♭	A	G		F			
2. Count:	1	2	3	4		1	2	3	4		1	2	3	4		1	2	3	4

FJH2217

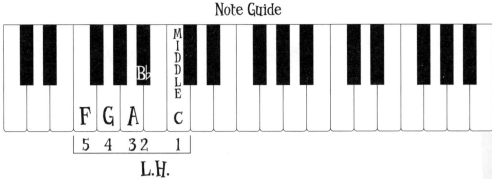

Note Guide

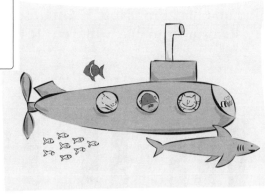

Submarine 🔘20

The B will stay flat if it is in the same measure.

Allegro

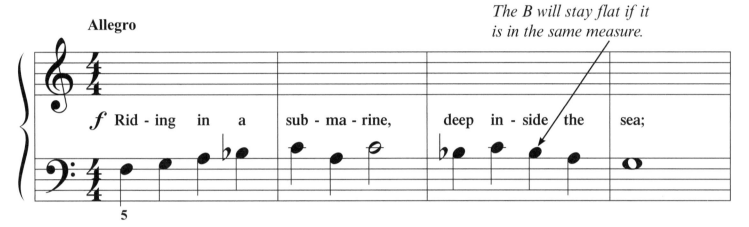

f Rid - ing in a | sub - ma - rine, | deep in - side the | sea;

5

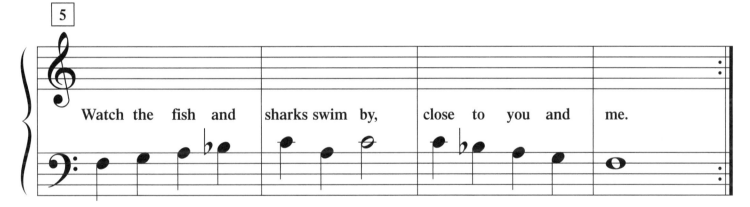

Watch the fish and | sharks swim by, | close to you and | me.

Teacher Duet: Student plays one octave higher.

mf with pedal

F Position Animals on the Treble Staff

FROG NOTE F, GIRAFFE NOTE G, ANACONDA A, BAT NOTE B FLAT, and COW NOTE C:
Find and play Frog Note F, Giraffe Note G, Anaconda A, Bat Note B Flat, and Cow Note C on your piano.
Remember to play with your R.H. finger 4 on the black key that sits just to the LEFT of Bat Note B.

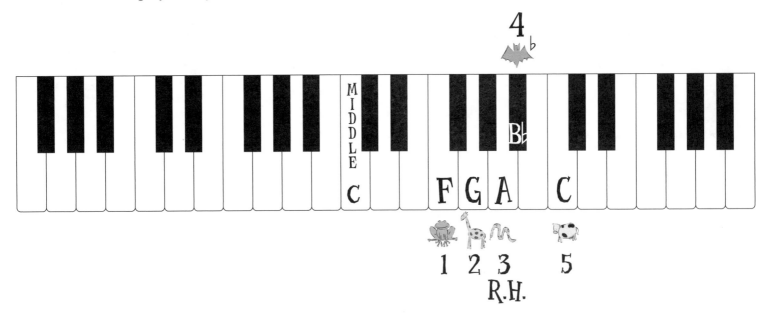

FROG NOTE F, GIRAFFE NOTE G, ANACONDA A, BAT NOTE B FLAT,
and COW NOTE C ON THE TREBLE STAFF:

Play the example below, keeping your eyes on the music.

	1	2	3	4	5												
1. Name notes:	F	G	A	Bb	C	Bb	A	G	F	G	A	Bb	C	A	F
2. Count:	1	2	3	4	1	2	3	4	1	2	3	4	1	2	3	4

FJH2217

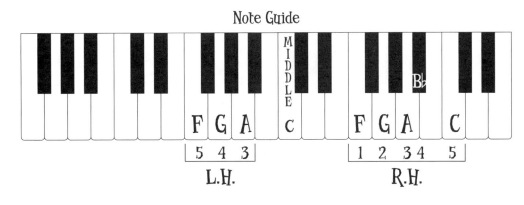

Note Guide

Hear the Wind 🔘21

Largo

mp Hear the wind | in the trees; | feel the cold and | chil - ly breeze.

5

See the wind | in the trees | rus - tle all the | leaves.

Teacher Duet: Student plays one octave higher.

R.H.

L.H. *p*

ped. simile

5

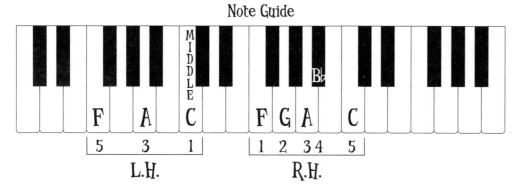

Note Guide

Ferris Wheel

Allegro

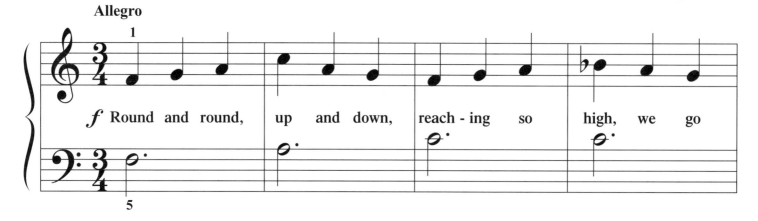

f Round and round, up and down, reach-ing so high, we go

up to the clouds on this Fer-ris wheel ride.

Teacher Duet: Student plays as written.

FJH2217

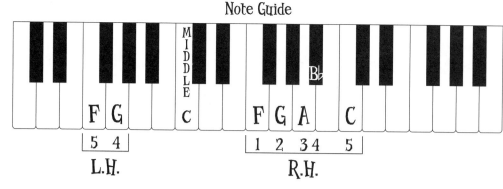

Note Guide

Huddle Close 23

Andante

mp Walk-ing through the for - est on a dark and wind - y night, We

hud - dle close to - geth - er as we see the creep - y sights.

Teacher Duet: Student plays as written.

D Hand Position . . .

The next group of notes in this book are in D Position. To play in D Position, place the left-hand finger number 5 on Duck Note D and finger number 3 on the BLACK KEY just to the RIGHT of Fish Note F. This note is called F sharp, but we will call it Fish Note F Sharp for fun. Place the right-hand thumb on Dog Note D and finger number 3 on the higher F sharp. We will call that note Frog Note F Sharp for fun. Place the rest of your fingers as indicated in the guide below.

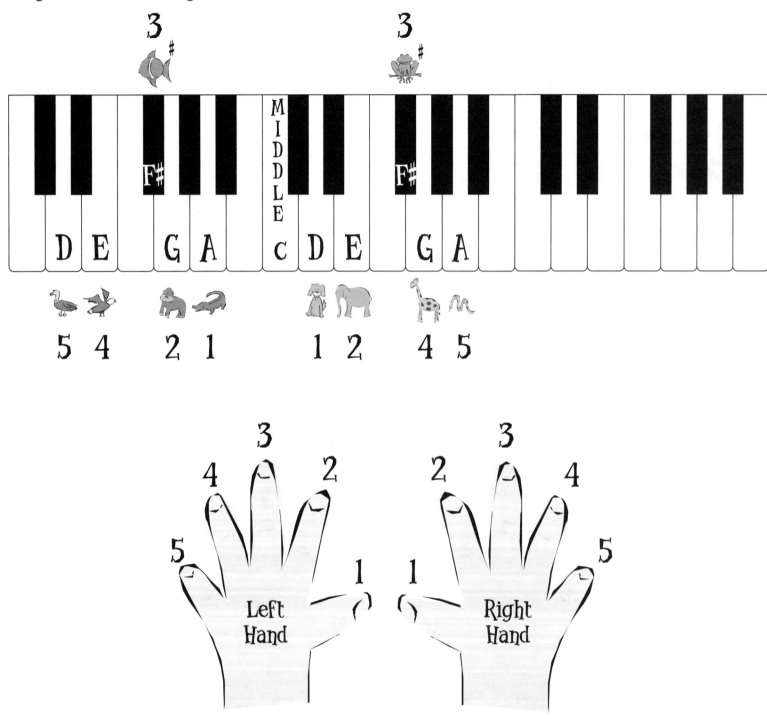

Remember hand positions are only "guides" that help you feel comfortable learning new notes. Once you are comfortable, your teacher can help you explore your pieces further by starting on a different finger.

Getting Comfortable in D Position . . .

Practice playing the notes in D Position. With one hand at a time, place your fingers in position, then play each note going up, then going down as shown with the animal pictures below. The finger numbers are there to guide you. You can play this as a warm-up every day for practice time at home. Try playing hands together when you feel ready.

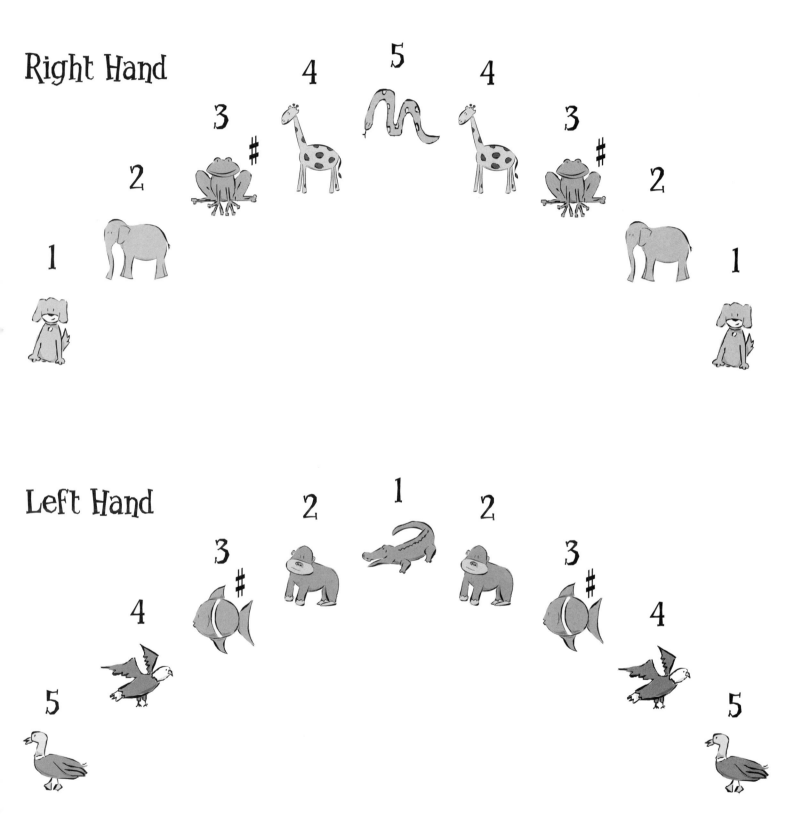

Theory Made FUN Sing-Along Book. Choose and review as desired.
Counting Made FUN Sing-Along Book. Choose and review as desired.
Notes Made FUN Sing-Along Book tracks 2-6, 15-19.

D Position Animals
on the Treble Staff

DOG NOTE D, ELEPHANT E, FROG NOTE F SHARP, GIRAFFE NOTE G, and ANACONDA A:
Find and play Dog Note D, Elephant E, Frog Note F Sharp, Giraffe Note G, and Anaconda A on your piano.
Remember to play with your R.H. finger 3 on the black key that sits just to the RIGHT of Frog Note F.

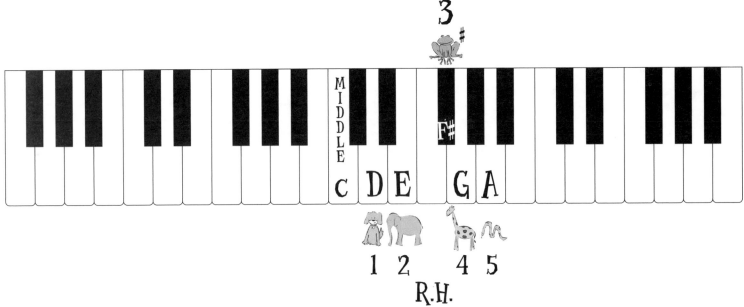

DOG NOTE D, ELEPHANT E, FROG F SHARP, GIRAFFE NOTE G, and ANACONDA A
ON THE TREBLE STAFF:

Play the example below, keeping your eyes on the music.

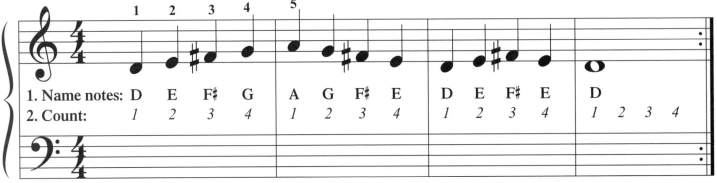

	1	2	3	4	1	2	3	4	1	2	3	4	1	2	3	4
1. Name notes:	D	E	F#	G	A	G	F#	E	D	E	F#	E	D			
2. Count:	1	2	3	4	1	2	3	4	1	2	3	4	1	2	3	4

FJH2217

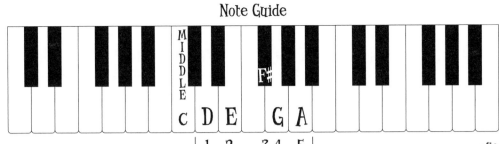

Note Guide

Glide as We Row

Andante

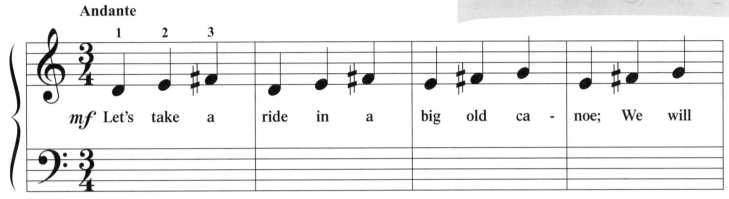

mf Let's take a   ride in a   big old ca - noe; We will

glide   as   we   row through the   rip - ples   so   blue.

Teacher Duet: Student plays as written.

FJH2217

D Position Animals on the Bass Staff

DUCK NOTE D, EAGLE NOTE E, FISH NOTE F SHARP, GORILLA NOTE G, and ALLIGATOR A:
Find and play Duck Note D, Eagle Note E, Fish Note F Sharp, Gorilla Note G, and Alligator A on your piano.
Remember to play with your L.H. finger 3 on the black key that sits just to the RIGHT of Fish Note F.

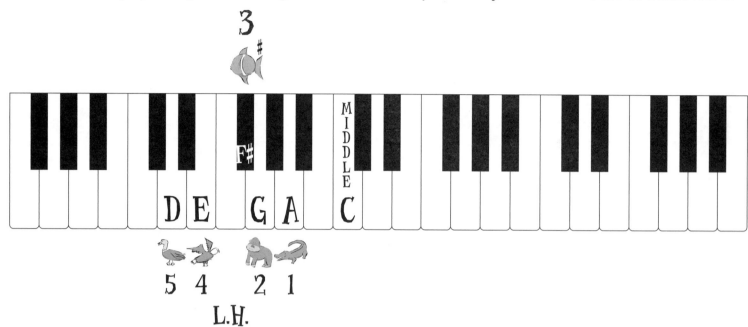

DUCK NOTE D, EAGLE NOTE E, FISH NOTE F SHARP, GORILLA NOTE G, and ALLIGATOR A
ON THE BASS STAFF:

Play the example below, keeping your eyes on the music.

| 1. Name notes: | D | E | F♯ | G | | A | F♯ | A | F♯ | | A | G | F♯ | E | | D | D | D | |
| 2. Count: | 1 | 2 | 3 | 4 | | 1 | 2 | 3 | 4 | | 1 | 2 | 3 | 4 | | 1 | 2 | 3 | 4 |

Clap to the Music 25

Andante

f Clap, clap to the mu - sic, lis - ten to the stead - y beat;

Clap, clap, to the mu - sic, turn and stomp your feet.

Teacher Duet: Student plays as written.

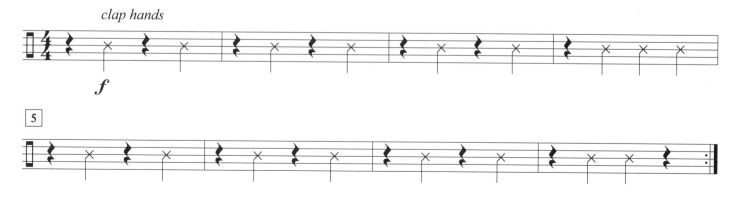

clap hands

f

Note Guide

Bubbles 26

Allegro

mp Bub - bles fly high, up to the sky;

When played as a solo, press the right
(damper) pedal for the entire piece.

Some - times they pop and I just don't know why.

Teacher Duet: Student plays as written.

Play 8va higher throughout

FJH2217

Note Guide

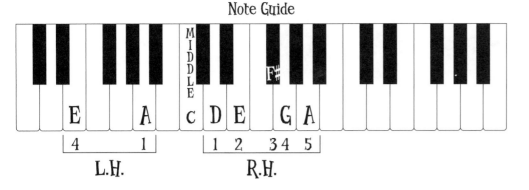

Shimmer Through the Light 🔘27

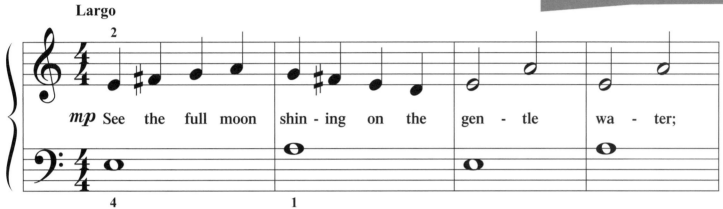

Largo

mp See the full moon shin - ing on the gen - tle wa - ter;

Watch the rip - ples shim - mer through the light. _____

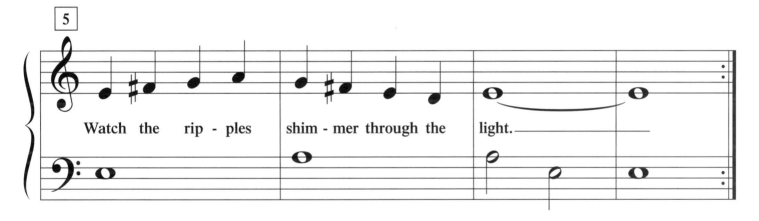

Teacher Duet: Student plays one octave higher.

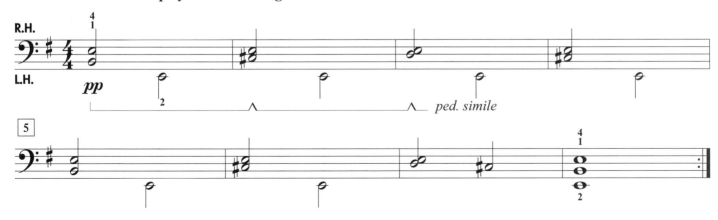

pp _____ *ped. simile*

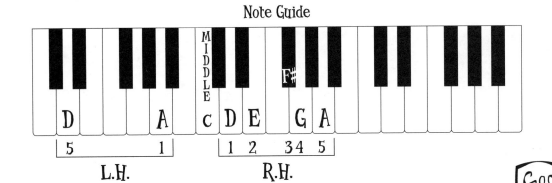

Note Guide

Time to Say Goodbye 28

Andante

Time to say good - bye, let's gath - er, ev - 'ry - one;

5

Time to say good - bye, we've had a lot of fun.

Teacher Duet: Student plays one octave higher.

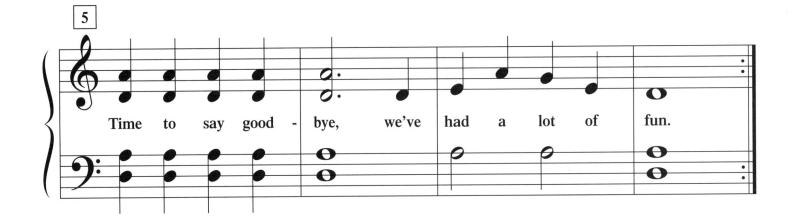

R.H.

L.H.

mf

5

On these pages, you could practice writing your notes, or even try writing your own songs.
You can also print more of these pages at **www.PianoMadeFun.com**.

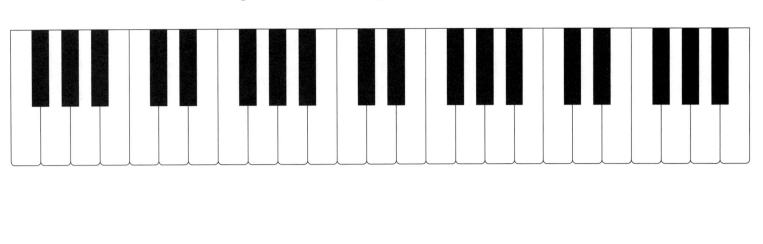

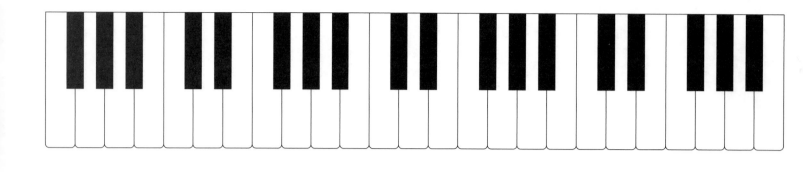

FJH2217

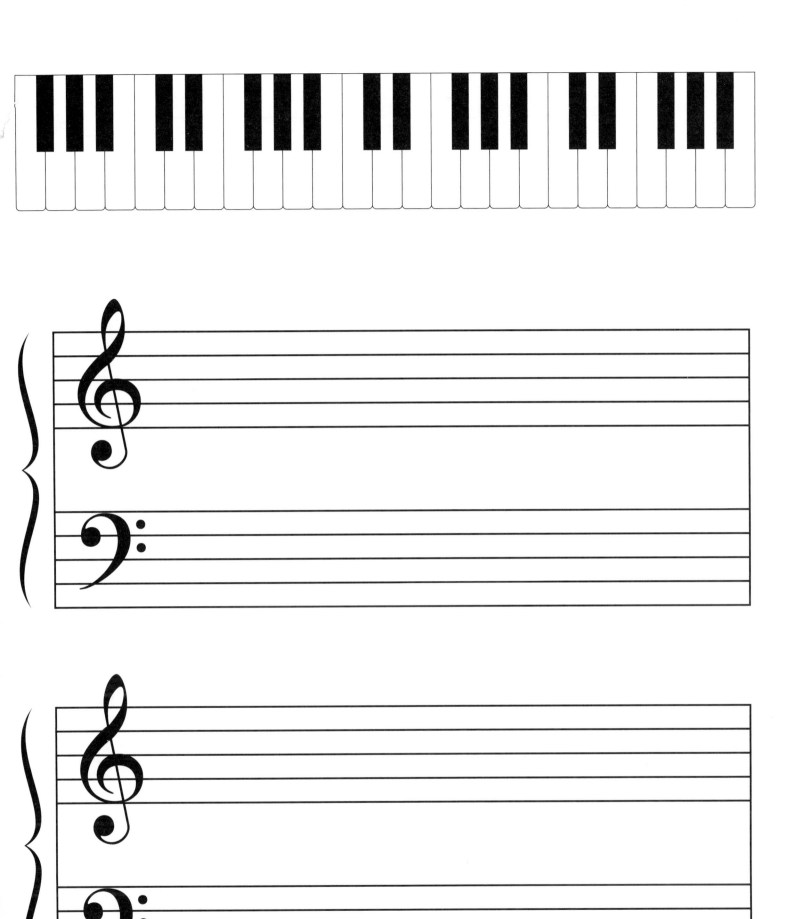

_____

Student

Congratulations!
You have now completed the

Note Reading Made FUN

Book 3

THE
F·J·H
MUSIC
COMPANY
INC.

Frank J. Hackinson

_____   _____

Date   Teacher's Signature